THE FUNDED TRADER'S
PLAYBOOK

THE ULTIMATE GUIDE FOR ASPIRING PROP FIRM TRADERS

KRON JENESIS

Risk Disclosure

Futures trading contains substantial risk and is not for every investor. An investor could potentially lose all or more than the initial investment. Risk capital is money that can be lost without jeopardizing ones' financial security or lifestyle. Any information in this book is neither a solicitation nor an offer to Buy/Sell futures, evaluation accounts, or funded accounts. No representation is being made that any account will or is likely to achieve profits or losses similar to those discussed in this book. Only risk capital should be used for trading and only those with sufficient risk capital should consider trading. Past performance is not necessarily indicative of future results.

Trading Evaluation Disclaimer

This book and its author, Kron Jenesis, does not guarantee that anyone will pass a prop firm evaluation. The overall pass rate for the funding firms (prop firms) will vary, but they are not easy to pass. The trading evaluation is a realistic simulation of trading under actual market conditions and is difficult to pass even for experienced traders. Trading evaluations are not suggested for individuals with minimal trading experience. You must conduct your own research into every funding firm prior to signing up with them. Kron Jenesis cannot be held liable for your performance or any dispute at all with prop firms. Every prop firm contains their own rules and regulations that you must adhere to, and it is your responsibility to know what they are and follow them.

Copyright © 2024, by Kron Jenesis.

All rights reserved. This book may not be reproduced in whole or in part, or transmitted in any form, without written permission from the author, except by a reviewer who may quote brief passages in a review; nor may any part of this book be reproduced, stored in a retrieval system, or transmitted in any form or by any means electronic, mechanical, photocopying, recording, or other, without written permission from the author.

BRICKELLTRADER

Follow Kron Jenesis on YouTube

@Brickelltrader

Website:

Brickelltrader.com

Thank You

A very special thank you to MCR, without you this book would not have been possible.

About the Author

Kron Jenesis, recognized by the formidable alias, The White Tiger, stands as a luminary figure in the realm of professional day trading, where the futures market becomes his strategic playground. Armed with a profound understanding of market dynamics and years of hands-on experience, Kron orchestrates trades with finesse and precision.

His journey through the volatile landscape of the financial markets is nothing short of awe-inspiring. Kron's unique approach to day trading unveils a tapestry of calculated risk-taking and insightful decision-making. A trailblazer in the futures market, The White Tiger not only embraces the challenges of this dynamic environment but thrives amidst its unpredictability.

From the early morning pre-market rituals to the closing bell drama, Kron navigates the ebb and flow of the futures market with an unwavering commitment to excellence, discipline, and above all…Capital Protection. His success story is etched in the highs and lows of countless trades, each contributing to the mosaic of his illustrious career.

In a world where milliseconds can make a difference, Kron emerges as a master of timing and strategy. His reputation for discerning market trends and capitalizing on opportunities not only underscores his position as a respected authority but also elevates him to a league of his own in the sophisticated world of day trading.

Contents

Introduction: Understanding Prop Firms   3

Types of Prop Firms   4

- Profit-sharing models.
- Evaluation to Funded.

How Prop Firms Operate   5

- Funding processes.
- Trading rules and restrictions.
- Payout structures.

Chapter 1: Researching Prop Firms   7

Identifying Credible Prop Firms   8

- Research strategies (forums, reviews, social media).
- Red flags to avoid (e.g., unrealistic promises, lack of transparency).

Evaluating Prop Firm Offers   9

- Comparing fee structures, payout ratios, and capital offers.

- Assessing trading platforms and tools provided.

Typical Evaluation Criteria   11

- Profit Targets
- Drawdown Limits

Chapter 2: The Evaluation Process   16

The Evaluation Process Explained   17

- Step-by-step guide to typical prop firm evaluations.
- What firms look for during the evaluation.

Common Mistakes to Avoid   18

- Psychological pitfalls (e.g., overtrading, revenge trading).
- Common technical errors and how to avoid them.

Strategies for Success   21

- Risk management techniques.
- Adapting your trading strategy for the evaluation phase.
- Maintaining discipline and consistency.

Chapter 3: Copy Trading & Managing Multiple Accounts   25

What is Copy Trading? 26

- Definition and concept.
- Manual vs. automated copy trading.

Benefits of Copy Trading and Managing Multiple Accounts 26

- Diversification of strategies.
- Time efficiency.
- Access to more capital.

Challenges and Considerations 32

- Monitoring performance across multiple accounts.
- Dealing with different trading conditions.
- Compliance with firm-specific rules

Chapter 4: Overcoming Psychological Barriers 36

Common Psychological Barriers 37

- Fear of failure.
- Performance anxiety.
- Imposter syndrome.

Strategies to Overcome Barriers 40

- Develop and follow a strong trading plan.

- Use mindfulness and stress management techniques.
- Focus on process over outcome.

Build Confidence — 42

- Practice in simulated environments.
- Manage risk and embrace losses.
- Build a support network.

Chapter 5: Mastering Position Sizing and Risk Management — 47

Understanding Position Sizing — 48

- Importance of controlling risk per trade.
- Why you shouldn't base position size on the nominal account value.
- How to properly size positions based on drawdown limits.

How to Properly Size Up Positions — 51

- Gradual position sizing based on account growth.
- Reassessing position size based on market conditions and volatility.
- Adjusting for volatility and market conditions.

Effective Risk Management Strategies — 52

- Using stop losses for every trade.
- Monitoring drawdown levels and scaling down when necessary.
- Diversifying trades and using risk management tools.

Chapter 6: Thinking in Probabilities   **57**

Thinking in Probabilities   **59**

- Understanding probabilistic thinking in trading.
- Applying probability concepts to trading decisions.

Building a Probabilistic Mindset   **61**

- Developing a mindset for long-term success.
- Utilizing probability to make informed trading choices.

Chapter 7: Building a Successful Trading Strategy   **65**

Developing a Trading Plan   **66**

- Components of a solid trading plan.
- Setting goals and objectives.

Strategy Optimization   **69**

- Backtesting and refining strategies.
- Adapting strategies to market conditions.

Performance Monitoring   **71**

- Tracking and evaluating performance.
- Making data-driven adjustments.

Chapter 8: Life After Passing   75

What Happens After You Pass   **76**

- Transitioning from the evaluation phase to live trading.
- Managing the capital and expectations.

Long-Term Success with a Prop Firm   **77**

- How to maintain consistency and grow your account.
- Building a career as a prop trader.

Scaling Up   **79**

- Strategies for increasing your capital and maximizing profits.
- Handling larger accounts and increased responsibilities.
- Key takeaways for finding and succeeding with a prop firm.

Chapter 9: The Future and Evolution of Prop Trading   83

The Shift in Prop Trading Models   **84**

- Moving away from evaluations as the main strategy.
- Prop firms shifting focus to immediate funding options.
- Higher initial costs, greater opportunities.

Adapting to Market Changes and Strategies 86

- Embracing new prop firm models.
- Financial planning for higher costs.
- Prioritize consistency and invest in continuous education.

Embracing Change and Growth 86

- Stay adaptive and consistent.
- Your journey is ongoing; you are capable of greatness.

Final Thoughts 92

A Little More About the Author 94

THE FUNDED TRADER'S PLAYBOOK

PREFACE

Welcome to the exhilarating world of day trading through proprietary firms, where ambition and opportunity converge in a fast-paced financial landscape. I'm Kron Jenesis, known in the trading community as The White Tiger, a passionate trader who thrives in the complexities of the futures market.

In this book, we will explore the intricate world of prop trading, shedding light on the structures, strategies, and psychological nuances that define this unique arena. Proprietary firms are pivotal in the trading ecosystem, offering traders access to significant capital and invaluable resources that can elevate their trading game. Unlike retail trading, where individuals often navigate with limited resources, prop firms provide a supportive environment for skilled traders to flourish. Here, you can leverage the firm's capital, benefit from robust risk management practices, and engage in invaluable training—key ingredients for success in the competitive realm of day trading.

Throughout our journey together, you'll uncover the compelling reasons to consider joining a prop firm, from enhanced risk management to valuable mentorship. However, it's equally crucial to recognize the potential challenges that may arise. This book is designed to equip you with the knowledge and tools necessary to navigate these complexities effectively.

Each chapter builds upon the last, beginning with the basics of prop firms and how they operate, and advancing through vital topics such as evaluation processes, risk management strategies, and the psychological hurdles traders often face. You'll learn not just how to select the right prop firm for your needs, but how to thrive within its framework.

Whether you're a newcomer eager to enter this world or an experienced trader looking to sharpen your strategies, this book is your comprehensive guide to mastering day trading in proprietary firms. Let's embark on this exciting journey and unlock the potential that lies ahead in this vibrant and rewarding field.

INTRODUCTION TO PROP FIRMS

Proprietary trading firms, commonly known as "prop firms," are companies that provide traders with the capital they need to trade in financial markets. In exchange, these firms take a share of the profits generated by the traders, or collect an upfront fee for the purchase of evaluations accounts or straight to sim-funded accounts. Prop firms have become an increasingly popular option for day traders looking to amplify their trading potential without risking their own capital. Understanding how these firms operate and what they offer is the first step in determining whether this path is right for you.

The Specific Type of Prop Firm We Discuss in This Book

1. Profit-Sharing Model

In the profit-sharing model, prop firms allocate a certain amount of capital to traders, who then trade using the firm's resources. Traders are not required to put up their own money, but instead, they earn a percentage of the profits they generate. This percentage can vary widely between firms, typically ranging from 50% to 90% of the profits. But traders must adhere to strict risk trading rules to avoid being let go from the firm.

Example:

- **Firm A:** Offers an 80/20 profit split in favor of the trader. The firm provides $50,000 in capital, and the trader's job is to generate profits while staying within the firm's risk parameters.

2. Evaluation to Funded

The initial evaluation is a subscription-based stage in your journey to become a funded trader. The firms charge traders a monthly fee to access their platforms, tools, and capital. Instead of taking a percentage of the profits, these firms earn revenue from the subscription fees. Traders are often given more autonomy in their trading decisions during the evaluation phase, but they still must adhere to the firm's risk guidelines.

Example:

- **Firm B:** Charges a $150 monthly fee for access to $50,000 in trading capital. The trader does not keep any profits because this is essentially a simulated account. However, if the trader passes the evaluation, they are provided the opportunity to trade a sim-funded account with the firm. The trader must pay the subscription fee regardless of performance, and then a fee for the sim-funded account.

How Prop Firms Operate

Prop firms function by leveraging their collective capital to empower individual traders, who then trade on behalf of the firm. The firm's revenue comes from either a share of the profits, subscription fees, funded account fees, or a combination of all three. To minimize risk, these firms set strict rules and guidelines for their traders. These rules typically include daily and overall drawdown limits, profit targets, consistency, and restrictions on the types of assets that can be traded.

Key Components of Prop Firm Operations:

- **Funding Processes:** Traders are usually required to pass an evaluation phase. This phase tests the trader's ability to follow the firm's rules while demonstrating profitable trading skills. Upon passing the evaluation, the trader receives a sim-funded account, also known as a PA Account, which stands for performance account. Traders are able to make profit withdrawals from this account.

- **Trading Rules and Restrictions:** To protect their capital, prop firms enforce risk management rules. These rules can include maximum position sizes, daily loss limits, and restrictions on holding positions overnight.
- **Payout Structures:** Depending on the firm, payouts can be daily, weekly, bi-weekly, or monthly. Traders may also be subject to payout thresholds, meaning they must reach a certain profit level before being eligible for a payout. And the payouts are usually capped depending on the account size.

Conclusion

Understanding the different types of prop firms, how they operate, and what to look for is the foundation for finding the right firm for your trading career. In the next chapter, we will dive deeper into the research process, providing strategies and tips for identifying credible prop firms and evaluating their offers.

CHAPTER 1
RESEARCHING PROP FIRMS

Introduction

Finding the right prop firm can make or break your trading career. With so many options available, it's crucial to conduct thorough research to identify credible firms that align with your trading goals and style. This chapter will guide you through the process of researching prop firms, evaluating their offers, and avoiding potential pitfalls.

Identifying Credible Prop Firms

The first step in your research is to identify prop firms that are reputable and trustworthy. Not all prop firms are created equal, and unfortunately, the industry has its share of bad actors. Here's how to spot the credible ones:

1. Start with Community Insights

The trading community is a valuable resource for gathering insights about different prop firms. Traders often share their experiences, both good and bad, on forums, social media platforms, and review sites. By reading these firsthand accounts, you can get a sense of which firms have a solid reputation and which ones to avoid.

Popular Resources:

- **Social Media:** YouTube, Twitter, Reddit, and Discord groups often have active discussions about prop firms.
- **Review Sites:** Websites like Trustpilot can provide additional insights into a firm's reputation.

2. Look for Transparency

A credible prop firm will be transparent about its fees, rules, and expectations. Be wary of firms that are vague or evasive about their terms. Legitimate firms usually provide detailed information on their websites about how they operate, including their funding process, evaluation criteria, and payout structures.

Key Indicators of Transparency:

- **Detailed FAQ Sections:** A firm's website should have a comprehensive FAQ section that answers common questions about the firm's operations.
- **Clear Contract Terms:** Before signing up, ensure that you have access to and understand the firm's contract. The terms should be clear, with no hidden fees or ambiguous clauses.

Evaluating Prop Firm Offers

Once you've identified a list of credible prop firms, the next step is to evaluate their offers. Different firms cater to different types of traders, so it's important to find a firm whose offers align with your specific needs and trading style.

1. Compare Fee Structures

Fee structures can vary widely between prop firms. Some firms charge upfront evaluation fees, while others may have ongoing subscription fees. It's crucial to understand what you're paying for and how those fees might impact your profitability.

Types of Fees to Consider:

- **Evaluation Fees:** These are often one-time or monthly fees paid when you sign up for the firm's evaluation process. The cost can range from a few hundred to a few thousand dollars, depending on the account sizes and the quantity of accounts purchased.
- **Sim-funded account Fees:** Firms charge a one-time or monthly fee for this type of account.
- **Profit Splits:** This refers to the percentage of profits the firm takes. Higher profit splits in favor of the trader are usually better, but they might come with stricter rules.

2. Assess Trading Platforms and Tools

The quality of a prop firm's trading platform can significantly affect your performance. Make sure the platform is reliable, user-friendly, and equipped with the tools you need to succeed.

Platform Features to Evaluate:

- **Execution Speed & reliability:** Fast execution is critical, especially for day traders who rely on quick trades. Same goes for the reliability of the software used to execute trades.
- **Charting Tools:** Advanced charting tools help in analyzing market trends and making informed decisions.
- **Customization:** The ability to customize the platform to your trading style can be a major advantage.

3. Evaluate Capital Offers

The amount of capital a firm provides is a crucial consideration. However, more capital isn't always better. You need to ensure that the capital offered aligns with your risk tolerance and trading strategy.

Considerations:

- **Scaling Potential:** Some firms offer more capital as you prove your profitability, allowing you to scale up your trading over time.
- **Drawdown Limits:** Understand the firm's drawdown policies, as they can affect how much risk you can take.

4. Understand the Evaluation Process

Most prop firms require traders to pass an evaluation before they can trade a sim-funded account or live capital. Understanding the evaluation process is essential for preparing effectively.

Typical Evaluation Criteria:

- **Profit Targets:** The firm may require you to reach a specific profit target within a given period.

- **Drawdown Limits:** Exceeding these limits can disqualify you from the evaluation process.
- **Trading Days:** Some firms require a minimum number of trading days to ensure consistent performance.
- **Consistency:** Some firms require you to stay at or below a specific consistency with regard to profits. I.e., no one day's profit may be more than 20% of any other day's profit.

Case Study: Evaluating Prop Firms

To illustrate the process of evaluating prop firms, consider the following case study involving a trader named Danny:

1. Defining Needs

Danny is a trader who requires moderate leverage, flexible risk management, and access to robust analytical tools. His goal is to generate consistent returns with manageable risk.

2. Research and Shortlisting

Danny conducts research and shortlists several prop firms based on his criteria. He focuses on firms that offer capital allocation suitable for his trading style, provide advanced analytical tools, and have reasonable risk management rules.

3. Evaluating Terms and Resources

Danny evaluates the terms and conditions of each firm on his shortlist. He compares capital allocation, leverage, risk management rules, and available resources. He also assesses the quality of educational materials and resources.

4. Asking Key Questions

Danny contacts the firms and asks key questions about profit-sharing structures, subscription fees, risk management rules, and support services. He seeks clarification on any terms and doesn't shy away from asking anything on which he requires further clarification.

5. Testing Platforms

Danny tests the trading platforms offered by the firms using demo accounts or just 1 trading account. Danny assesses the functionality, user experience, and compatibility with his trading strategies.

6. Making a Decision

Based on his evaluation, Danny selects a prop firm that provides the best combination of capital allocation, support, and flexibility for his trading style.

Conclusion

Researching and evaluating prop firms is a critical step in your journey as a day trader. By identifying credible firms, comparing their offers, and understanding the evaluation process, you can make an informed decision that aligns with your trading goals.

Chapter 1 – Recap

- Thorough research is essential to finding a prop firm that aligns with your trading goals.
- Use community insights from forums and review sites to identify reputable firms.
- Credible firms are transparent about fees, rules, and expectations on their websites.
- Compare evaluation, subscription fees, and profit splits to find the best offer.
- Ensure the trading platform is reliable, fast, and equipped with useful tools.
- Consider the firm's capital offers, scaling potential, and drawdown limits.
- Understand the evaluation process, including profit targets and trading day requirements.
- Ask firms key questions about terms, profit-sharing, and support services.
- Testing platforms and resources can help you make an informed decision.
- Choose a firm that aligns with your trading style, risk tolerance, and needs.

CHAPTER 2

THE EVALUATION PROCESS

Introduction

The evaluation process is the gateway to accessing live capital from a prop firm. It's a rigorous test of your trading skills, discipline, and ability to manage risk. In this chapter, we'll break down the evaluation process, common mistakes to avoid, and strategies to assist you during the evaluation phase.

The Evaluation Process Explained

Prop firms use the evaluation process to assess whether a trader is capable of consistently generating profits while adhering to strict risk management rules. Understanding the structure of this process is crucial for success.

1. Stages of Evaluation

Most prop firms have a multi-stage evaluation process that typically includes:

- **Initial Evaluation Stage:** This stage tests your ability to meet profit targets while respecting drawdown limits. You may be required to trade over a specified period (e.g., 20 trading days) and achieve a certain profit margin without breaching the firm's risk parameters.
- **Sim-Funded Account Stage:** If you pass the initial evaluation, the sim-funded account stage confirms your consistency. The targets might be more demanding than the initial stage, but the emphasis is on demonstrating that you can sustain your trading performance. This is the final hurdle before receiving full access to the firm's live capital.
- **Live Account Test:** After passing both the initial and sim-funded stages, you may be offered an opportunity to trade the firm's live capital.

2. Key Evaluation Criteria

Understanding what the firm expects during the evaluation can help you tailor your approach:

- **Profit Targets:** Firms set specific profit goals that traders must achieve. These targets vary depending on the firm and the capital size.
- **Drawdown Limits:** Maximum allowable losses (daily and overall) are strictly enforced. Exceeding these limits typically results in immediate disqualification.
- **Trading Days:** Many firms require traders to trade for a minimum number of days to demonstrate consistent performance. You can't just hit the profit target quickly and stop; consistency is key.
- **Risk Management Rules:** Firms often have additional rules, such as limiting position sizes, restricting certain trading hours, or prohibiting specific assets. This may vary greatly from firm to firm.

Common Mistakes to Avoid

The evaluation process can be challenging, and many traders fail not because of a lack of skill, but due to avoidable mistakes. Here are some common pitfalls and how to steer clear of them:

1. Overtrading

Overtrading is one of the most common reasons traders fail evaluations. The pressure to hit profit targets can lead to taking too many trades, which increases the likelihood of making errors.

How to Avoid:

- **Stick to Your Plan:** Only take trades that meet your pre-defined criteria. Avoid the temptation to enter trades out of impatience or fear of missing out.
- **Set a Daily Limit:** Define the maximum number of trades you'll take each day and stick to it.

2. Revenge Trading

Revenge trading occurs when traders try to quickly recover losses by taking impulsive trades. This emotional response can quickly spiral out of control and lead to significant drawdowns.

How to Avoid:

- **Take a Break:** If you experience multiple losses and feel that you are on tilt, step away from your trading station. Give yourself time to cool down before considering another trade.
- **Focus on the Long Game:** Remember that the evaluation is about consistency, not short-term gains. Accept losses as part of the process and move on.

3. Ignoring Risk Management Rules

Ignoring the firm's risk management rules is a surefire way to fail an evaluation. Whether it's exceeding position sizes or holding trades longer than allowed (swing trades/past market close), breaking these rules shows a lack of discipline.

How to Avoid:

- **Know the Rules Inside Out:** Make sure you fully understand the firm's rules before you start trading. Keep a checklist if needed.
- **Use Stop-Loss Orders:** Always set stop-loss orders to ensure that you stay within the firm's drawdown limits.

4. Neglecting Psychology

The mental aspect of trading is often overlooked, but it plays a crucial role in the evaluation process. Stress, anxiety, and overconfidence can all lead to poor decisions.

How to Avoid:

- **Practice Mindfulness:** Techniques like meditation or deep breathing can help you stay calm and focused during the evaluation.
- **Stay Detached:** Try to remain emotionally detached from each trade. Focus on the process rather than the outcome.

Strategies for Success

Passing the evaluation requires more than just avoiding mistakes; it demands a strategic approach. Here are some proven strategies to help you succeed:

1. Risk Management Techniques

Proper risk management is the cornerstone of passing the evaluation. Here's how to implement it effectively:

- **Position Sizing:** Use a position-sizing formula that aligns with the firm's drawdown limits. For example, risking 1-2% of your account per trade is a common approach.
- **Stop-Loss Placement:** Place stop-loss orders at logical levels based on technical analysis. Ensure your stops align with the firm's rules.
- **Reward: Risk Ratio:** Aim for a ratio of at least 2:1. This means you should be targeting twice the amount (or more) you risk on each trade.

2. Adapting Your Trading Strategy

Your regular trading strategy might need adjustments to fit the evaluation criteria. Here's how to adapt:

- **Tighten Your Strategy:** During the evaluation, focus on high-probability setups. Avoid risky trades that don't clearly meet your criteria.
- **Manage Your Expectations:** Don't aim for unrealistic returns. It's better to consistently hit smaller profits than to swing for the fences and risk blowing up.
- **Backtest:** Before starting the evaluation, backtest your strategy under conditions similar to what the evaluation requires. This can help you fine-tune your approach.

3. Maintaining Discipline and Consistency

Discipline and consistency are the two most critical factors for passing the evaluation. Here's how to maintain them:

- **Follow a Routine:** Establish a daily routine that includes pre-market analysis, trading, and post-market review. Consistency in your routine will translate to consistency in your trading.
- **Journal Your Trades:** Keep a detailed trading journal to track your performance, mistakes, and improvements. Reviewing your journal regularly can help you stay disciplined and learn from your experiences.
- **Stay Patient:** Remember, the evaluation process is a marathon, not a sprint. Don't rush to meet profit targets. Focus on consistent, disciplined trading over time.

Conclusion

Passing a prop firm's evaluation process is a challenging but achievable goal. By understanding the evaluation criteria, avoiding common mistakes, and implementing effective strategies, you can position yourself for success. The key is to stay disciplined, manage risk, and maintain a consistent approach throughout the process.

Chapter 2 – Recap

- The evaluation tests your trading skills, risk management, and consistency for access to a sim-funded account.
- Most firms have 3 stages: evaluation, sim-funded, and live account access,
- Key criteria include meeting profit targets, staying within drawdown limits, and completing minimum trading days.
- Overtrading and revenge trading can lead to failure in the evaluation.
- Ignoring risk management rules shows a lack of discipline.
- Managing psychological aspects like stress and overconfidence is vital for success.
- Effective risk management involves position sizing, stop-loss placement, and a solid risk/reward ratio.
- Adapt your strategy by focusing on high-probability setups and avoiding unnecessary risks.
- Maintaining discipline through a routine and trade journaling increases your chances of passing.
- Patience and a long-term focus on consistent trading are key for evaluation success.

CHAPTER 3
COPY TRADING & MANAGING MULTIPLE ACCOUNTS

Introduction

In the fast-paced world of day trading, efficiency and diversification are key to long-term success. One of the strategies gaining popularity among traders is copy trading, which allows you to replicate trades across multiple accounts simultaneously. This approach can be particularly advantageous when managing accounts with different prop firms, as it not only streamlines the trading process but also maximizes the benefits that come with diversification.

This chapter will explore the concept of copy trading, the benefits of managing multiple accounts with different prop firms, and how these strategies can lead to increased profitability. We'll also provide real-life examples to illustrate the potential advantages of this approach.

What is Copy Trading?

Copy trading is a method that allows traders to replicate the trades they make in one account across multiple other accounts. This can be done manually or through automated software, enabling traders to manage several accounts simultaneously without having to execute each trade individually.

How Copy Trading Works

The core principle of copy trading is simple: when you place a trade in one account, the same trade is automatically mirrored in other accounts linked to it. This is made possible through specialized trading platforms or software that connect multiple accounts and ensure that every trade is executed identically across them.

For instance, if you initiate a long position on the E-mini Nasdaq in your primary account, the same position will be opened in all other connected accounts with the exact same parameters—entry price, stop-loss, and take-profit levels. This synchronization is particularly useful when you're managing accounts with different prop firms, each offering varying conditions and capital allocations.

Benefits of Copy Trading Across Multiple Accounts

Copy trading offers several advantages, especially when managing accounts across multiple prop firms. These benefits can significantly enhance your trading efficiency, reduce risk, and ultimately lead to greater profitability.

1. Diversification of Strategies

One of the primary benefits of copy trading is the ability to diversify your trading strategies across multiple accounts. By employing different strategies in different accounts, you can hedge against the risk of any single strategy failing.

Example: Imagine you have three accounts with different prop firms. In one account, you follow a trend-following strategy; in another, you use a mean-reversion approach; and in the third, you focus on breakout trading. By copy trading, you can replicate the most successful trades across all accounts, effectively blending the strengths of each strategy. This diversification reduces the overall risk and increases the chances of consistent profitability.

2. Time Efficiency

Managing multiple accounts manually can be time-consuming and prone to errors. Copy trading simplifies this process by allowing you to execute trades once and have them automatically replicated across all connected accounts.

Example: Suppose you trade during volatile market conditions, where speed and precision are crucial. Instead of entering the same trade separately in five different accounts, you can place the trade in your primary account, and the copy trading software will ensure that the same trade is executed instantly in all other accounts. This not only saves time but also ensures that you don't miss out on opportunities due to the delay of manual execution.

3. Consistency and Discipline

Copy trading promotes consistency in your trading decisions, as all accounts will follow the same trades without deviation. This consistency is vital for maintaining discipline, especially when emotions run high during market fluctuations.

Example: A trader managing accounts with varying sizes and conditions may be tempted to trade differently based on the account balance or firm's rules. However, with copy trading, the same disciplined approach is applied uniformly, minimizing the risk of overtrading or deviating from the strategy due to emotional impulses.

Benefits of Trading with Multiple Prop Firms

Trading with multiple prop firms offers additional benefits beyond what you can achieve with a single firm. These advantages, when combined with copy trading, can significantly enhance your trading potential.

1. Risk Diversification

By spreading your trading activities across multiple prop firms, you reduce the risk associated with being tied to a single firm. Different firms have different rules, capital allocation, and stability, so diversifying across several firms protects you from unexpected changes or issues with any one firm.

Example: Consider a situation where one prop firm suddenly changes its drawdown policy, making it more stringent. If you're trading with multiple firms, this change will only affect a portion of your trading capital, while the rest remains unaffected, allowing you to continue trading with less disruption.

2. Access to More Capital

Each prop firm offers its own capital allocation. By passing evaluations with multiple firms, you can significantly increase the total capital available to you for trading. This allows you to take larger positions, potentially increasing your profit potential.

Example: Suppose you have accounts with three different prop firms, each offering $15,000 in trading capital. By managing these accounts simultaneously, you effectively have $45,000 in capital to work with. This larger capital base allows you to scale your positions and target higher returns without increasing your risk per trade. (Note: Capital refers to the amount of money you can lose. I.e., a nominal $150,000 account with a 5% maximum drawdown is essentially a $7,500 account with approximately $150,000 in buying power.)

3. Leveraging Different Firm Benefits

Different prop firms have varying benefits, such as profit splits, drawdown rules, and platform features. By trading with multiple firms, you can take advantage of these differences to optimize your trading strategy.

Example: Firm A might offer a more generous profit split, while Firm B has more lenient drawdown rules, and Firm C provides access to better trading tools. By trading with all three, you can allocate trades strategically to maximize your overall profit and minimize risk based on the strengths of each firm.

4. Reducing Dependency on a Single Firm

Relying on a single prop firm can be risky, especially if the firm faces financial difficulties or changes its terms in a way that negatively impacts your trading. By spreading your accounts across multiple firms, you mitigate the risk of being overly dependent on any one firm.

Example: If a prop firm you're trading with suddenly goes out of business or changes its payout structure, your entire trading career could be jeopardized if that's your only firm. However, if you're working with multiple firms, the impact of such an event is less severe, as you still have other accounts to continue trading.

Profitable Examples: Copy Trading vs. Not Copy Trading

To better illustrate the potential benefits of copy trading and managing multiple accounts, let's look at two scenarios: one where a trader uses copy trading and another where they do not.

Example 1: Using Copy Trading

A trader, Alex, manages three accounts with different prop firms. In each account, Alex follows a different trading strategy: momentum trading in Account A, zone fades in Account B, and scalping in Account C. By using copy trading, Alex can replicate the best trades from each strategy across all three accounts.

In a given month, the momentum strategy performs exceptionally well, yielding a 30% return in Account A. Thanks to copy trading, the same trades are executed in Accounts B and C. Meanwhile, the zone fades and scalping strategies provide moderate returns, but the overall performance is boosted by the successful momentum trades replicated across all accounts.

Result: Alex's total return across all accounts is higher than if each account had followed a single strategy without copying the successful trades from the others.

Example 2: Not Using Copy Trading

Now, let's consider another trader, Jamie, who also manages three accounts with different prop firms but does not use copy trading. Jamie employs the same strategies as Alex but keeps each account isolated, with no trades being replicated.

In the same month, Jamie's momentum strategy in Account A yields a 50% return, but the other strategies in Accounts B and C only provide a 10% return each. Without the benefit of copying the successful momentum trades, Jamie's overall performance is lower, as the gains from the momentum strategy are confined to a single account.

Result: Jamie's total return is less diversified and lower overall compared to Alex's, illustrating the potential advantage of using copy trading to maximize profits across multiple accounts.

Challenges and Considerations

While copy trading and managing multiple accounts offer significant benefits, they also come with challenges that must be addressed to ensure success.

1. Monitoring Performance Across Multiple Accounts

Keeping track of performance across multiple accounts can be complex. Traders must use effective tools to monitor and analyze performance, ensuring that all accounts are performing as expected and that any issues are promptly identified.

2. Dealing with Different Trading Conditions

Different prop firms may offer varying spreads, execution speeds, and asset availability. Adjusting your strategy to fit these conditions while maintaining consistency can be challenging but is essential for optimizing performance.

3. Payout and Fee Management

Managing payouts, fees, and commissions across multiple firms requires careful planning. Traders must be aware of the different cost structures of each firm to ensure that fees do not eat into profits.

4. Compliance with Firm-Specific Rules

Each prop firm has its own rules and requirements, which can be challenging to keep track of when managing multiple accounts. It's crucial to understand and comply with these rules to avoid disqualification or loss of funding.

Conclusion

Copy trading and managing multiple accounts across different prop firms can be a powerful strategy for day traders looking to diversify their risk, increase efficiency, and maximize profitability. While this approach comes with its own set of challenges, the potential rewards make it a valuable option for traders who are willing to put in the effort to manage it effectively. By leveraging the benefits of different firms and synchronizing strategies through copy trading, traders can achieve greater consistency and success in their trading endeavors.

Chapter 3 – Recap

- Copy trading lets traders replicate trades across multiple accounts at once.
- This can be done manually or through automated software for efficient management.
- When a trade is made in the primary account, it mirrors in all linked accounts with the same parameters.
- It helps diversify strategies, reducing the risk of any single strategy failing.
- Managing multiple accounts manually takes time, but copy trading simplifies execution for all accounts.
- Copy trading promotes consistent trading decisions as all accounts follow the same trades.
- Trading with multiple prop firms diversifies risk and reduces dependency on one firm.
- Passing evaluations with several firms increases total trading capital.
- Different firms offer unique benefits, and copy trading allows leveraging these differences.
- While copy trading has benefits, it also presents challenges like performance monitoring and compliance.

CHAPTER 4
OVERCOMING PHYCHOLOGICAL BARRIERS

Introduction

The path to becoming a successful trader with a prop firm is often filled with psychological challenges. Traders not only have to demonstrate their technical skills but also confront a variety of mental and emotional obstacles that can significantly impact their performance. The pressure of passing an evaluation, coupled with the fear of failure, can create psychological barriers that hinder even the most talented traders. In this chapter, we will explore the most common psychological challenges faced during prop firm evaluations and provide practical strategies to help traders overcome these barriers.

Common Psychological Barriers in Prop Firm Evaluations

1. Fear of Failure

The fear of failure is one of the most pervasive psychological barriers that traders face. When attempting to pass a prop firm evaluation, the stakes are high—often involving both financial commitments (such as evaluation fees) and the pressure of proving oneself capable of trading profitably with the firm's capital. This fear can lead to hesitation, indecision, and a lack of confidence in executing trades, ultimately impacting performance.

How It Manifests:

- Traders may become overly cautious, avoiding potentially profitable trades due to fear of loss.
- Alternatively, traders might overcompensate by taking excessive risks to achieve quick results, leading to emotional trading and mistakes.

2. Performance Anxiety

Performance anxiety occurs when traders feel overwhelmed by the need to perform at their best to pass the evaluation. The knowledge that their every trade is being monitored can heighten anxiety, causing them to second-guess their decisions or abandon their trading plan.

How It Manifests:

- Traders may experience increased stress, which can result in fatigue, irritability, and difficulty focusing.
- Anxiety may cause traders to exit trades too early or hold onto losing trades longer than they should, fearing that one loss could jeopardize their evaluation.

3. Imposter Syndrome

Many traders experience imposter syndrome, the feeling that they are not truly skilled or deserving of success, despite evidence of their competence. This can be particularly common among newer traders or those who have experienced setbacks in the past. Imposter syndrome can cause self-doubt, which may affect a trader's ability to stick to their strategy.

How It Manifests:

- Traders may hesitate to enter trades they otherwise believe in due to a lack of confidence.
- They might question their own abilities and constantly compare themselves to other traders, creating a sense of inadequacy.

4. Overtrading Due to Pressure

The desire to pass the evaluation quickly or meet specific profit targets can drive traders to overtrade. Overtrading often results from a psychological state where traders feel compelled to be in the market constantly, believing that more trades will increase their chances of success. This behavior can lead to impulsive, emotion-driven decisions rather than disciplined, strategic trading.

How It Manifests:

- Traders might enter trades with lower probability setups or engage in revenge trading after losses.
- Overtrading can also result in burnout, increased transaction costs, and the erosion of potential profits

5. Loss Aversion

Loss aversion is the tendency to prefer avoiding losses over acquiring equivalent gains. For many traders, the pain of losing money during an evaluation is greater than the satisfaction of making money. This psychological bias can lead to poor decision-making, such as closing trades prematurely to avoid any loss or refusing to cut a losing position in the hope that it will turn around.

How It Manifests:

- Traders might exit trades too soon, missing out on potential profits, or fail to use stop losses appropriately, letting losses run.
- Fear of incurring losses can lead to paralysis, where traders are unable to make any decision at all.

Strategies to Overcome Psychological Barriers

Overcoming these psychological barriers is essential for passing a prop firm evaluation. Below are practical strategies to help traders build mental resilience and develop the mindset needed to succeed.

1. Develop a Strong Trading Plan and Stick to It

A well-defined trading plan is the foundation of disciplined trading. It should include specific rules for entry and exit, risk management, position sizing, and profit-taking strategies. Having a plan provides a clear roadmap, reducing the likelihood of emotional decision-making.

How to Implement:

- **Create a Detailed Plan:** Outline your trading strategy, including which setups you will trade, under what conditions, and with what risk parameters. Make the plan specific and actionable.
- **Practice Discipline:** Commit to following your plan consistently, even when faced with losing trades or unexpected market conditions. This builds confidence in your strategy and reduces impulsive actions.
- **Regular Review:** Periodically review your plan and trading performance. Identify what is working and adjust if needed but avoid changing your plan after every loss.

2. Use Mindfulness and Stress Management Techniques

Mindfulness and stress management techniques can help traders stay calm and focused during evaluations. These practices improve self-awareness, allowing traders to recognize when they are acting out of fear or anxiety.

How to Implement:

- **Practice Mindfulness Meditation:** Set aside a few minutes each day to practice mindfulness meditation. Focus on your breathing and observe your thoughts without judgment. This can help you stay grounded during stressful situations.
- **Develop a Pre-Trading Routine:** Create a pre-trading routine that includes activities like deep breathing exercises, visualization, or positive affirmations to calm the mind and prepare for the trading day.
- **Manage Physical Health:** Regular exercise, a healthy diet, and sufficient sleep contribute to overall well-being, reducing stress levels and improving focus.

3. Focus on Process Over Outcome

Shifting focus from the outcome (i.e., passing the evaluation) to the process (i.e., executing your strategy correctly) can help reduce pressure and anxiety. By concentrating on what you can control—your actions, discipline, and decision-making—you become less fixated on the results of individual trades.

How to Implement:

- **Set Process-Oriented Goals:** Instead of setting goals based on profit or loss, set goals based on following your trading plan accurately. For example, aim to execute 10 trades following your strategy precisely, regardless of the outcome.
- **Reflect on Each Trade:** After each trading day, reflect on how well you adhered to your plan rather than focusing on the profit or loss. Identify any emotional decisions and work on minimizing them in future trades.

4. Build Confidence Through Simulated Practice

Simulated trading, or "paper trading," can help build confidence without the risk of real capital. This approach allows traders to test their strategies in a controlled environment and develop a sense of competence that can translate into the actual evaluation.

How to Implement:

- **Use Simulated Trading Platforms:** Choose a reputable platform that offers realistic market conditions for practice. Focus on applying your trading plan and managing your trades as if it were a real evaluation.

- **Set Realistic Expectations:** Treat simulated trading with the same seriousness as live trading. Use it to identify weaknesses in your strategy and work on your psychological responses to wins and losses.

5. Manage Risk and Embrace Losses as Part of the Process

Risk management is crucial in trading and understanding that losses are a natural part of the process can help reduce fear and anxiety. By managing risk effectively, traders can maintain emotional equilibrium even after a losing trade.

How to Implement:

- **Define Risk Parameters:** Set clear risk parameters for each trade, such as a maximum percentage of your account that you are willing to risk. This helps prevent significant losses and keeps emotions in check.
- **Use Stop Losses:** Always use stop losses to limit potential losses. This can help you avoid the temptation to hold onto losing trades longer than necessary.
- **Embrace Losses as Learning Opportunities:** Instead of viewing losses as failures, treat them as opportunities to learn and refine your strategy. Focus on understanding why a trade didn't work and how to improve in the future.

6. Build a Support Network

Having a support network of fellow traders, mentors, or a trading community can provide encouragement, advice, and perspective during challenging times. This sense of community can help traders feel less isolated and more resilient in the face of psychological challenges.

How to Implement:

- **Join Trading Communities:** Participate in online trading forums, groups, or social media communities where you can share experiences and gain insights from other traders.
- **Seek Mentorship:** Find a mentor or experienced trader who can provide guidance, feedback, and emotional support. A mentor can help you navigate the challenges of prop firm evaluations with greater confidence.
- **Engage in Peer Discussions:** Discuss your trading experiences, both successes and failures, with peers. Sharing your journey can help normalize setbacks and reduce feelings of inadequacy or isolation.

Conclusion

Passing a prop firm evaluation is not only a test of a trader's technical skills but also a challenge to their mental fortitude. Psychological barriers such as fear of failure, performance anxiety, imposter syndrome, overtrading, and loss aversion can significantly impact a trader's performance. However, by developing a strong trading plan, managing stress, focusing on process over outcome, managing risk, and building a support network, traders can overcome these challenges and increase their chances of success.

Ultimately, becoming a successful trader requires not just a mastery of the markets but also a deep understanding of oneself. By acknowledging and addressing psychological barriers, traders can cultivate the mindset needed to navigate the evaluation process with confidence and resilience.

Chapter 4 – Recap

- The path to becoming a successful trader is filled with psychological challenges.
- Common barriers include fear of failure, performance anxiety, and imposter syndrome.
- Fear of failure can lead to hesitation in trades and excessive risk-taking.
- Performance anxiety causes stress, leading traders to second-guess decisions.
- Imposter syndrome creates self-doubt and hesitance in executing trades.
- Overtrading results from the urge to constantly be in the market, leading to impulsive decisions.
- Loss aversion leads to avoiding losses at the expense of potential gains.
- Strategies to overcome these barriers include a strong trading plan and mindfulness.
- Building confidence through simulated trading can reduce fear during evaluations.
- A support network of traders or mentors helps navigate psychological challenges.

CHAPTER 5

MASTERING POSITION SIZING & RISK MANAGEMENT

Introduction

Position sizing and risk management are two of the most critical aspects of successful trading, especially when participating in prop firm evaluations. Many traders mistakenly believe that position size should be determined based on the nominal account size, such as $150,000, without taking into account the maximum drawdown limits imposed by the firm. This approach can lead to excessive risk-taking and rapid losses, jeopardizing the trader's chances of passing the evaluation. In this chapter, we will explore the principles of proper position sizing, how to scale positions effectively, and the best practices for managing risk based on the allowable drawdown rather than the total account size.

Understanding Position Sizing and Its Importance

Position sizing is the process of determining the number of contracts or lots to trade in any given position. The primary objective of position sizing is to control the amount of risk taken on each trade, ensuring that no single trade can significantly impact the overall capital or lead to a violation of the prop firm's drawdown limits.

Proper position sizing is crucial because it directly affects:

- **Risk Management:** Controls how much of the account is at risk on each trade.
- **Consistency:** Ensures that the trader can withstand a series of losses without depleting the account.
- **Psychological Stability:** Helps maintain emotional discipline by preventing oversized losses that could trigger fear, anxiety, or revenge trading.

Why You Shouldn't Base Position Size on the Nominal Account Value

Prop firms often provide traders with large nominal account values, such as $50,000, $100,000, or even $150,000. However, these figures can be misleading when it comes to determining position size because they do not reflect the actual amount of money that the trader can lose. Instead, most prop firms set specific drawdown limits that define the maximum allowable loss before the evaluation is failed or the account is closed.

Example: For a $150,000 prop firm account, the maximum drawdown might be $7,500. In this case, the trader should base their risk calculations and position sizing on the $7,500 drawdown limit rather than the full $150,000 account size. This approach ensures that the trader remains within the firm's risk parameters and significantly reduces the risk of breaching the drawdown limit.

How to Properly Size Your Positions

Proper position sizing begins with understanding the maximum risk you are willing to take on any single trade, usually expressed as a percentage of the allowable drawdown, not the nominal account size.

1. Determine the Maximum Risk Per Trade

A common rule of thumb is to risk no more than 1-2% of the total drawdown on any single trade. This means calculating the dollar amount of risk based on the maximum allowable drawdown.

How to Calculate Maximum Risk:

- **Determine the Drawdown Limit:** Identify the maximum drawdown allowed by the prop firm.

- **Set a Risk Percentage:** Decide the percentage of the drawdown you are willing to risk per trade. A conservative approach might be 1%, while a more aggressive trader may choose up to 2%.
- **Calculate the Dollar Risk:** Multiply the drawdown limit by the chosen risk percentage. For example, if the drawdown is $5,000 and you risk 1% per trade, your maximum risk per trade would be $50.

2. Calculate Position Size Based on Risk

Once you know your maximum risk per trade, the next step is to calculate the appropriate position size. This involves determining how many contracts or lots to trade based on the amount of risk you are willing to take.

- **Dollar Risk per Trade** is the maximum amount you are willing to lose on a trade (e.g., $50).
- **Stop Loss Distance** is the difference between the entry price and the stop loss price of the trade.

3. Adjust for Market Conditions and Volatility

Market conditions and volatility play a crucial role in determining position size. In highly volatile markets, a larger stop loss may be necessary to avoid being stopped out by normal price fluctuations. In such cases, reducing the position size can help manage risk while maintaining the same dollar risk per trade.

How to Adjust:

- **Wider Stop Loss = Smaller Position Size:** If the stop loss distance increases due to volatility, decrease the position size to keep the dollar risk constant.
- **Use Volatility Indicators:** Tools like the Average True Range (ATR) can help determine appropriate stop loss distances based on market volatility.

How to Properly Size Up Positions

As traders gain confidence and experience, they may consider increasing their position sizes to maximize profits. However, sizing up should be done cautiously and systematically to avoid taking on excessive risk.

1. Gradual Position Sizing

Instead of doubling or tripling your position size suddenly, increase your position size gradually as your account grows or as you demonstrate consistent profitability.

How to Implement:

- **Increase in Small Increments:** For example, increase your position size by 1 contract every time you achieve a specific profit milestone or after a certain number of consecutive profitable trades.

- **Maintain the Same Risk Percentage:** Even as you size up, continue to risk the same percentage (e.g., 1-2%) of the drawdown limit per trade. This approach allows you to scale up your position sizes while maintaining the same level of risk.

2. Reassess Position Size Regularly

Regularly reassessing your position size based on account growth, market conditions, and changes in volatility is essential for risk management.

How to Implement:

- **Review Weekly or Monthly:** Analyze your trading performance and account size on a weekly or monthly basis to determine if adjustments are needed.
- **Adapt to Changes in Drawdown:** If the maximum allowable drawdown increases or decreases (due to firm policy changes or account growth), adjust your position size accordingly.

Effective Risk Management Strategies

Effective risk management goes beyond position sizing. It involves developing a comprehensive strategy to manage drawdowns, prevent significant losses, and ensure consistent performance.

1. Use a Stop Loss for Every Trade

A stop loss is a predetermined price at which you will exit a losing trade to prevent further losses. Using a stop loss for every trade is a fundamental risk management practice.

How to Implement:

- **Set Stop Loss Based on Strategy:** Determine the appropriate stop loss level based on your trading strategy, market conditions, and the asset's volatility.
- **Adjust Stop Loss for Volatility:** In volatile markets, widen your stop loss to avoid being stopped out by normal price fluctuations but reduce position size to maintain the same dollar risk.

2. Monitor Drawdown Levels Closely

Staying within the allowable drawdown limits is crucial to passing a prop firm evaluation. Regularly monitor your drawdown levels and adjust your trading strategy if necessary to avoid breaching the limit.

How to Implement:

- **Track Drawdown Daily:** Keep a record of your drawdown levels daily to ensure you are not approaching the maximum allowed.

- **Scale Down if Needed:** If you are nearing the drawdown limit, consider reducing position size or taking a break from trading to reassess your strategy.

3. Diversify Your Trades

Diversifying your trades across different instruments, sectors, or asset classes can help reduce overall risk and prevent significant losses from a single position.

How to Implement:

- **Trade Multiple Assets:** Instead of concentrating all risk in one asset, consider trading multiple assets that are not highly correlated.
- **Limit Exposure to Any One Trade:** Set a maximum exposure limit for any single trade or asset class to avoid overconcentration of risk.

4. Use Risk Management Tools

Leverage risk management tools such as trailing stops and hedging strategies to protect your account from excessive losses.

How to Implement:

- **Trailing Stops:** Use trailing stops to lock in profits as the market moves in your favor while protecting against sudden reversals.
- **Hedging:** Consider using hedging strategies to offset potential losses in your primary trading positions. (Note: Hedging may be a rule violation, ensure that you verify with the firm beforehand.)

Conclusion

Proper position sizing and risk management are essential components of successful trading, especially when attempting to pass a prop firm evaluation. Traders must base their position sizes on the maximum allowable drawdown, not the nominal account size, to stay within the firm's risk parameters and avoid premature evaluation failure. By determining maximum risk per trade, adjusting for market conditions, sizing up cautiously, and implementing robust risk management practices, traders can build a strong foundation for sustainable trading success.

Understanding and applying these principles will help you maintain control over your trading account, prevent significant losses, and increase your chances of passing prop firm evaluations while developing a disciplined and resilient trading mindset.

Chapter 5 – Recap

- Position sizing and risk management are vital for successful trading in prop firm evaluations.
- Traders often misjudge position size based on nominal account values instead of drawdown limits.
- Proper position sizing controls risk, maintains consistency, and supports psychological stability.
- Don't base position size on account value; use drawdown limits to determine risk exposure.
- Maximum risk per trade should typically be 1-2% of the drawdown limit.
- Adjust position size based on market volatility and conditions to manage risk effectively.
- Increase position sizes gradually and reassess them regularly based on performance and market changes.
- Implement stop losses for every trade, monitor drawdown levels, and diversify trades to reduce risk.
- Mastering these principles enhances control over trading accounts and boosts the chances of passing evaluations.

CHAPTER 6
MASTERING YOUR EMOTIONS & THINKING IN PROBABILITIES

Introduction

In trading, success is not just about skill, strategy, or technical analysis—it's also about mastering the mind. Prop firms provide traders with an opportunity to manage larger sums of capital, but with this chance comes significant pressure. This pressure often leads to emotional and psychological challenges that can disrupt even the most well-prepared trading plan. Mastering your emotions and adopting probabilistic thinking is essential to navigating the high-stakes world of prop trading successfully. In this chapter, we'll explore how to think in probabilities to make informed trading decisions.

Mastering Emotions

Emotions are an inevitable part of trading but allowing them to dictate your actions is a surefire way to fail. Whether it's the euphoria from a winning streak or the crushing despair of a losing streak, emotions often lead to irrational decisions. Trading is a game of patience, resilience, and, most importantly, emotional control.

Identifying Emotional Triggers in Trading

The first step to mastering your emotions is identifying your emotional triggers. Each trader is different; some may be triggered by large wins, while others might feel anxious after a loss. Typical emotional triggers include:

- **Fear of Missing Out (FOMO):** FOMO leads traders to chase the market, entering trades too late and without solid reasoning. It's an emotional reaction to seeing a price move without you being a part of it.
- **Fear of Loss:** Fear can paralyze you or make you exit a trade prematurely. This emotion often stems from past losses or fear of losing the capital you've worked hard to accumulate.
- **Greed:** Greed occurs when traders push for more profit than their strategy allows, often holding on to winning trades too long, resulting in the reversal of gains.

- **Revenge Trading:** After a loss, the urge to "win back" what was lost often leads to taking ill-advised, high-risk trades. It's an emotional reaction rather than a logical decision.

By understanding and acknowledging these emotional triggers, you can prepare yourself to manage them when they inevitably arise.

Thinking in Probabilities

A core principle in successful trading is the understanding that no single trade defines your success. Each trade is simply one outcome in a long series of probabilistic events. The moment you stop thinking in certainties and start thinking in probabilities, you're on the path to long-term success.

Understanding Probabilistic Thinking in Trading

Probabilistic thinking involves recognizing that the outcome of any given trade is uncertain and subject to random factors. Even a perfectly executed trade setup could result in a loss. Conversely, a trade that goes against your rules might result in a profit. However, this does not mean that you should abandon your strategy when trades go wrong. Instead, it means you must think in terms of probabilities rather than guarantees.

When you adopt probabilistic thinking, you stop being attached to the outcome of individual trades. Instead, you evaluate your performance over a large sample of trades. For example, a strategy that has a 60%-win rate will inevitably have 40% losing trades. Knowing this allows you to accept losses without becoming emotional, as they are part of the process.

Applying Probability Concepts to Trading Decisions

Once you accept that every trade is subject to probability, you can start applying this thinking to your decisions. Here's how:

- **Reward:Risk Ratio:** When placing a trade, always calculate your potential profit versus your potential loss. A good reward/risk ratio ensures that even if you lose more trades than you win, you can still be profitable. For example, if you're stand to make $300 and risk only $100, you only need to win one out of three trades to break even.
- **Win Rate and Sample Size:** Understand your strategy's win rate. If you know that your system has a win rate of 50%, you can expect one out of every two trades to be profitable. However, this doesn't mean that profits and losses will alternate perfectly—sometimes you'll have streaks of losses or wins. What matters is the consistency of the strategy over a large sample size.
- **Expected Value (EV):** This is the statistical expectation of how much you can expect to win or lose per trade, on average, over time. It's calculated by multiplying the probability of a win or loss by the expected gain or loss for each outcome. If your EV is positive, you have a statistical edge in the market.

- **Accepting Randomness:** Understand that randomness plays a significant role in the outcome of individual trades. Just as a coin toss can land heads or tails regardless of previous results, the market can sometimes act unpredictably. Don't let short-term randomness distract you from executing a long-term plan.

By applying these probability concepts to your trading, you start viewing each trade not as a win-or-lose event, but as part of a larger system that, when executed properly, should result in long-term profitability.

Building a Probabilistic Mindset

Building a probabilistic mindset requires both psychological and practical adjustments to how you approach the market. It is not enough to understand probability—you must internalize it to the point that it informs every trade you make.

Developing a Mindset for Long-Term Success

Long-term success in prop trading is built on the idea that you will not win every trade, and that's okay. Instead, success depends on executing a strategy consistently, knowing that over time, the probabilities will work in your favor.

- **Detaching from Individual Outcomes:** Detach yourself emotionally from the outcome of individual trades. This can be challenging, but you must trust the statistical edge of your

system. Instead of focusing on each win or loss, focus on how well you followed your process.
- **Avoiding Overconfidence:** Winning streaks can lead to overconfidence, which is just as dangerous as fear. Stick to your strategy regardless of recent performance. Probabilities remain constant over time, and outliers in performance (both good and bad) will occur.

Utilizing Probability to Make Informed Trading Choices

Once you've internalized probabilistic thinking, you'll be in a better position to make informed decisions.

- **Trading with a Plan:** Always have a clear plan that includes your entry, exit, and stop-loss points, based on probabilistic analysis. This removes emotional decision-making and helps you stick to your strategy.
- **Managing Risk Consistently:** Risk management is about controlling the downside while letting the upside play out over time. Use probability to determine the appropriate size of each trade relative to your account.

By understanding and embracing probabilistic thinking, you set yourself up for a more objective and strategic approach to trading. Instead of relying on hope or fear, you rely on data, systems, and the law of large numbers to guide your decisions.

Conclusion

Mastering your emotions and thinking in probabilities are two sides of the same coin when it comes to successful prop trading. While emotions can cloud judgment, probabilistic thinking can provide clarity and structure. Together, these skills enable you to manage risk, stay disciplined, and ultimately succeed in the long run. In the world of trading, the edge goes to those who can control their emotions and think strategically in terms of probabilities rather than certainties.

Chapter 6 – Recap

- Success in trading involves mastering emotions alongside skill and strategy.
- Emotional challenges can disrupt even the best trading plans.
- Identify emotional triggers like FOMO, fear of loss, greed, and revenge trading.
- Thinking in probabilities means recognizing that individual trades don't define success.
- Use reward:risk ratios and understand win rates to inform trading decisions.
- Accept randomness and detach from outcomes to improve consistency.
- Build a probabilistic mindset focused on long-term execution over short-term results.
- Always trade with a clear plan and manage risk consistently.
- Mastering emotions and thinking probabilistically together leads to trading success.

CHAPTER 7
BUILDING A SUCCESSFUL TRADING STRATEGY

Introduction

There's a saying in the car industry, "it's not the car, it's the driver." Well, the same goes for trading, it's not the strategy, it's the trader. Meaning, you may have a profitable strategy, but if you don't have the proper mindset, you will not execute the strategy effectively. Any real trader will agree to this. And it's primarily the reason why this chapter is towards the end of the book and why I drilled in on the psychology and mindset required to achieve success prior to this chapter. Not because it's not less important, having a good strategy, an edge in the market, is required to succeed in this game. But your mindset is what will carry you through times of drawdowns and the inevitable adversity that will come your way, time and time again.

In the world of prop trading, your success largely hinges on having a well-thought-out, adaptable trading strategy. Without a structured approach, even the most experienced traders can find themselves at the mercy of the markets. A solid trading strategy is not only your roadmap to profitability but also a key to managing risk and ensuring long-term success. In this chapter, we'll explore how to develop a comprehensive trading plan, optimize your strategies, and monitor your performance to stay ahead in the competitive prop trading space.

Developing a Trading Plan

A trading plan is a blueprint that outlines how you will navigate the market. It provides structure and consistency to your trading activities, ensuring that each decision is aligned with your overall goals. While every trader's plan will vary based on personal preferences, risk tolerance, and market focus, there are core components that every effective plan must include.

Components of a Solid Trading Plan

A well-constructed trading plan has several essential elements:

- **Market Selection:** The first step in creating a trading plan is deciding which markets or instruments you will trade. Whether it's forex, futures, or any other market, selecting one that suits your style and risk appetite is crucial. Consider factors like liquidity, volatility, and trading hours.
- **Trading Style:** Your trading style—whether it's swing trading or scalping, it should be based on your availability, experience level, and personality. Scalping requires intense focus and fast decision-making, while swing trading allows for a longer timeframe and more flexibility. There are many other trading styles to choose from.

- **Risk Management:** Defining your risk tolerance is one of the most critical aspects of any trading plan. Establish rules for how much capital you are willing to risk per trade, as well as your maximum drawdown tolerance. Many successful traders adhere to the 1-2% rule, risking no more than 1-2% of their account on any single trade.
- **Entry and Exit Criteria:** Establish specific criteria for entering and exiting trades. This can include technical indicators, chart patterns, price levels, or a combination of factors. Clear entry and exit rules prevent impulsive decisions driven by emotion.
- **Position Sizing:** Position sizing refers to determining how much of your capital you will allocate to each trade. This should be calculated based on your risk tolerance and the reward/risk ratio of the trade. Keeping your positions appropriately sized can prevent significant losses during volatile periods.
- **Reward/Risk Ratio:** A good trading plan includes a predetermined reward/risk ratio for each trade. This ratio measures how much you stand to make for the risk you stand to lose. A common rule is to aim for a minimum of a 2:1 reward-to-risk ratio, meaning that you expect to earn $2 for every $1 you risk. I personally strive to achieve a 5:1 for the majority of my trades.
- **Stop-Loss and Take-Profit Levels:** Stop-loss orders automatically close a trade when it reaches a certain level of loss, protecting your capital from excessive losses. Similarly, take-profit levels automatically lock in profits when the market

hits a predetermined price point. Both are essential to executing disciplined trades.
- **Psychological Preparedness:** Trading is a mentally taxing activity, and a robust trading plan accounts for your mental and emotional state. Include guidelines for how you'll handle losing streaks, winning streaks, and periods of market uncertainty.

Setting Goals and Objectives

Setting clear, measurable goals is critical to staying focused and motivated in your trading career. When setting goals, think of both long-term and short-term objectives.

- **Short-term Goals:** These can include daily or weekly targets, such as making a certain number of trades or achieving a specific percentage return. However, it's important to keep your goals realistic and attainable. Unrealistic expectations can lead to overtrading or taking on excessive risk.
- **Long-term Goals:** Consider where you want to be as a trader in six months, a year, or five years. Long-term goals may involve scaling up your account size, passing a number of prop firm evaluations, or transitioning from part-time to full-time trading. These goals should reflect the broader vision of your trading career.

Both types of goals provide a roadmap for improvement, helping you stay accountable to your trading plan while fostering a mindset of growth and resilience.

Strategy Optimization

Once you have developed a trading plan, the next step is optimizing your strategy to ensure it performs well across various market conditions. Optimization is an ongoing process that requires constant refinement and adjustment. Traders who consistently optimize their strategies increase their chances of long-term success.

Backtesting and Refining Strategies

Backtesting is a process that involves applying your trading strategy to historical market data to evaluate its performance. It allows you to assess how your strategy would have performed under different conditions without risking real capital. When done correctly, backtesting provides critical insights into the strengths and weaknesses of your strategy.

- **Choosing Reliable Data:** Ensure that you're using high-quality, reliable data for backtesting. Inaccurate data can lead to faulty conclusions, so it's essential to use historical data from reputable sources.
- **Testing a Large Sample Size:** To accurately gauge your strategy's effectiveness, you need to test it over a large sample

size. A small number of trades won't give you a clear picture of your strategy's true performance. Aim for at least 100 trades to get statistically significant results.

- **Simulating Different Market Conditions:** A good strategy must be flexible enough to perform well under various market conditions, including bull markets, bear markets, and periods of consolidation. Test your strategy across different timeframes and market environments to see how it holds up.
- **Refining the Strategy:** After backtesting, it's time to refine your strategy based on the results. Adjust entry and exit rules, position sizing, and risk management criteria if necessary. The goal is to maximize profitability while minimizing risk.
- **Avoiding Over-Optimization:** While it's tempting to tweak a strategy until it performs perfectly on historical data, this often leads to over-optimization, or "curve-fitting." A curve-fitted strategy may perform well in backtesting but poorly in real-time trading because it's too tailored to past data. Focus on developing a robust strategy rather than one that fits historical patterns too perfectly.

Adapting Strategies to Market Conditions

Market conditions are always changing, and a strategy that works in one environment may struggle in another. Successful traders recognize the importance of adapting their strategies to different market dynamics.

- **Volatility Adjustments:** Volatility can significantly impact the performance of a trading strategy. During periods of high volatility, price movements can be erratic, increasing the likelihood of stop-losses being triggered. In contrast, low volatility can lead to slow, choppy markets that offer few trading opportunities. Adjust your position sizing and stop-loss levels based on the current volatility of the market.
- **Market Trends:** Understanding the prevailing trend in the market is crucial for adjusting your strategy. In a strong uptrend, it may make sense to use trend-following strategies, while in a ranging market, mean-reversion strategies might be more effective. Be flexible and ready to switch strategies when market conditions shift.
- **Timeframe Considerations:** Different timeframes present different challenges. Shorter timeframes like 1-minute or 5-minute charts require quick decision-making and can be more volatile. Longer timeframes, such as daily or weekly charts, provide more time for analysis but may miss short-term price movements. Adjust your strategy to the timeframe that aligns with your trading goals and lifestyle.

Performance Monitoring

Building a successful trading strategy isn't just about planning and optimization—it's also about consistently monitoring performance. Tracking your performance allows you to identify areas for improvement and make necessary adjustments to stay profitable over the long run.

Tracking and Evaluating Performance

Performance tracking is an essential part of ensuring your trading strategy remains effective. Without thorough tracking, it's easy to lose sight of what's working and what isn't.

- **Trade Journal:** One of the best ways to monitor your performance is by maintaining a detailed trading journal. Record every trade, including entry and exit points, the rationale behind the trade, the outcome, and your emotional state during the trade. This documentation allows you to review your decisions and identify patterns in both your wins and losses.
- **Metrics to Track:** Keep an eye on key performance metrics, such as win rate, reward/risk ratio, maximum drawdown, and average profit per trade. These metrics give you a comprehensive view of how your strategy is performing..

Making Data-Driven Adjustments

When your performance starts to decline, resist the temptation to make impulsive changes based on a few losing trades. Instead, rely on data-driven adjustments.

- **Identifying Weak Points:** Analyze your trading journal and performance metrics to identify weak points in your strategy.

Are there specific market conditions where your strategy struggles? Do you tend to make emotional decisions after a series of losses? Pinpointing the cause of poor performance is the first step in making effective adjustments.

- **Testing Adjustments:** When you identify areas for improvement, test any adjustments through backtesting or in a demo account. Avoid making significant changes to your live trading strategy until you've tested the impact of those adjustments.

- **Continuous Improvement:** Trading is a continuous learning process, and even the most successful traders make regular adjustments to their strategies. Commit to a process of ongoing improvement, using data and performance metrics to guide your decisions.

Conclusion

Building a successful trading strategy requires careful planning, consistent optimization, and diligent performance monitoring. By developing a comprehensive trading plan, optimizing your strategies based on backtesting and market conditions, and regularly tracking your performance, you can set yourself up for long-term success in the world of prop trading. Remember, trading is not about perfection—it's about consistently refining your process to improve your edge over time.

Chapter 7 – Recap

- Trading success hinges on mindset, not just strategy.
- A solid strategy is crucial for risk management.
- Key elements: market selection, trading style, and entry/exit rules.
- Set clear short-term and long-term trading goals.
- Refine strategies through backtesting and market adaptation.
- Use quality data and a large sample for evaluations.
- Adjust for volatility, trends, and timeframe.
- Keep a trade journal to track performance.
- Make data-driven adjustments, not emotional ones.
- Continuously refine your process to improve your edge.

CHAPTER 8
LIFE AFTER PASSING

Introduction

Congratulations! Passing the evaluation process is a significant achievement, but it's just the beginning of your journey as a prop trader. Now, the real challenge begins: managing live capital and consistently generating profits while navigating the unique dynamics of trading with a prop firm. In this chapter, we'll explore what happens after you pass the evaluation, how to maintain long-term success, and strategies for scaling up your trading.

What Happens After You Pass

After successfully passing the evaluation, you'll transition from the evaluation phase to trading a sim-funded account where you can make withdrawals on your profits. This transition comes with its own set of challenges and opportunities.

1. Transitioning to Live Trading

Trading sim-funded account (PA account) can feel different from trading in the evaluation phase, even if the mechanics are the same. The psychological pressure of trading this type of account can affect decision-making and risk management.

Key Considerations:

- **Emotional Adjustment:** Be prepared for the psychological shift when trading with a sim-funded account. Stay calm and maintain the discipline you developed during the evaluation.
- **Sticking to Your Strategy:** Resist the temptation to deviate from the strategy that got you through the evaluation. If it worked then, it should work now.
- **Risk Management:** Continue to prioritize risk management. The firm's drawdown limits will still apply, and it's crucial to protect your capital.

2. Managing the Capital and Expectations

Once you start trading a sim-funded account, it's important to manage both your trading and your expectations.

Considerations:

- **Start Slow:** Don't rush into making large trades. Start with smaller positions as you get used to the new account and the pressures that come with it.
- **Focus on Consistency:** The firm will have a record of your performance. Focus on consistent profitability rather than trying to hit home runs.
- **Payouts and Reinvestments:** Understand the firm's payout structure. Some traders choose to reinvest a portion of their profits into buying more accounts to grow their capital base.

Long-Term Success with a Prop Firm

Achieving long-term success as a prop trader requires more than just passing the evaluation; it demands continuous learning, adapting to market conditions, and maintaining a disciplined approach.

1. Continuous Learning and Adaptation

The markets are constantly evolving, and what worked yesterday might not work tomorrow. To stay successful, you need to keep learning and adapting your strategies.

Strategies for Continuous Learning:

- **Market Analysis:** Regularly analyze market conditions and adjust your trading strategies accordingly. Stay informed about global economic events and trends that could impact the markets.
- **Education:** Invest in your education by reading trading books, attending webinars, and engaging with the trading community. Learning from others' experiences can provide valuable insights.
- **Review and Reflect:** Periodically review your trading journal to identify areas for improvement. Reflecting on your trades helps you understand what's working and what needs adjustment.

2. Managing Stress and Avoiding Burnout

The life of a prop trader can be stressful, especially when dealing with the pressure to perform consistently. Managing stress and avoiding burnout are crucial for long-term success.

Tips for Managing Stress:

- **Work-Life Balance:** Don't let trading consume your entire life. Make time for hobbies, exercise, and social activities to maintain a healthy work-life balance.
- **Stress Management Techniques:** Practice stress management techniques such as meditation, deep breathing, or mindfulness to stay calm during trading sessions.

- **Regular Breaks:** Take regular breaks from trading to recharge. This can prevent burnout and help you maintain focus when you return to the markets.

3. Building a Career as a Prop Trader

For many, passing the evaluation is just the first step toward building a long-term career as a prop trader. Here's how to establish yourself in the industry:

Networking and Community Engagement:

- **Join Trading Communities:** Engaging with other traders can provide support, new ideas, and opportunities for collaboration.
- **Attend Conferences:** Consider attending trading conferences or seminars to network with other professionals in the industry.
- **Mentorship:** If possible, find a mentor who has experience in the industry. A mentor can offer guidance and help you navigate the challenges of a trading career.

Scaling Up

As you gain confidence and experience, scaling up your trading can lead to higher profits and greater opportunities within the firm.

1. Strategies for Increasing Your Capital

Many prop firms offer the opportunity to increase your capital allocation as you demonstrate consistent profitability. Here's how to approach scaling up:

Incremental Growth:

- **Prove Consistency First:** Before asking for more capital, prove that you can manage your current allocation effectively and profitably over a sustained period.
- **Negotiate Capital Increases:** If your firm doesn't automatically increase your capital, consider negotiating for a higher allocation based on your performance.
- **Use Profits to Scale:** Some traders reinvest a portion of their profits into their trading account to gradually increase their position sizes and potential returns.

2. Handling Larger Accounts

Trading with a larger account requires a different mindset and approach. The stakes are higher, and the potential for both profit and loss increases.

Key Considerations:

- **Risk Management:** As your account grows, so does the importance of strict risk management. Larger positions mean larger potential losses, so it's crucial to stay disciplined.
- **Emotional Control:** Trading with larger sums can amplify emotions. Stay detached and continue to make decisions based on logic and strategy rather than fear or greed.
- **Diversification:** Consider diversifying your trades across different assets or strategies to spread risk and reduce the impact of any single loss.

Conclusion

Passing the evaluation is just the beginning of your journey as a prop trader. The real challenge lies in maintaining consistency, managing stress, and scaling up your trading while navigating the complexities of trading with live capital. By focusing on continuous learning, disciplined risk management, and strategic growth, you can build a successful and sustainable career in prop trading. In the next chapter, we'll discuss how to handle setbacks and challenges in your trading journey, ensuring that you stay on track to achieve your long-term goals.

Chapter 8 – Recap

- Passing the evaluation is just the start; live trading presents new challenges.
- Adjust emotionally when transitioning to trading with real capital.
- Stick to the strategy that got you through the evaluation.
- Start with small trades to build confidence in the live environment.
- Focus on consistent profitability rather than large wins initially.
- Commit to continuous learning and market adaptation for long-term success.
- Manage stress through work-life balance and stress relief techniques.
- Network with other traders and seek mentorship for career growth.
- Scale up trading by proving consistency before requesting more capital.
- Practice strict risk management and emotional control with larger accounts.

CHAPTER 9

THE FUTURE & EVOLUTION OF PROP TRADING

Introduction

As we stand on the brink of a new era in prop trading, the landscape is shifting beneath our feet. The traditional structures that have defined this industry are evolving, offering new opportunities and challenges for traders. In this chapter, we will explore the significant changes occurring in prop trading models, how traders can adapt to these transformations, and an inspirational message to empower day traders as they navigate their journeys.

The Shift in Prop Trading Models

The first major change in the prop trading landscape is the movement away from evaluation-based models. Historically, prop firms have utilized rigorous evaluation processes as a primary marketing strategy. Traders seeking funding had to demonstrate their skills by passing these evaluations, often under significant psychological pressure. While this model provided a way for firms to vet potential traders, it also created barriers that could discourage talent and limit access to funding.

Moving Away from Evaluations as the Main Strategy

The drawbacks of the evaluation system are becoming increasingly apparent. For many traders, particularly those with experience, the pressure to pass a simulation can lead to performance anxiety and poor decision-making. As the prop trading industry evolves, firms are recognizing that they can attract and retain talent by eliminating this hurdle.

This shift is a response to the changing needs of traders who prefer immediate access to capital. Many experienced traders feel that they shouldn't have to prove their abilities through simulations when they have a track record of consistent performance. Prop firms are beginning to cater to this demographic by designing programs that prioritize direct funding, thereby streamlining the entry process.

Prop Firms Shifting Focus to Immediate Funding Options

As prop firms move away from evaluations, they are increasingly offering immediate funding options. These programs allow traders to access real capital right away, which can be a game-changer for those looking to maximize their trading potential.

Immediate funding options provide a quicker pathway to profitability. Traders no longer need to endure a lengthy evaluation process; instead, they can start executing trades with real money from the get-go. This approach is not only appealing to experienced traders but also to newer traders who may be eager to begin their careers without the barrier of a simulated test.

Higher Initial Costs, Greater Opportunities

While immediate funding options are attractive, they often come with higher upfront costs. Traders may find themselves facing more significant fees to access these funding programs. However, the demand for these types of offerings is likely to grow, as many traders recognize that the potential for higher earnings outweighs the initial investment.

The higher costs associated with immediate funding programs reflect the value of immediate access to capital. For traders who can demonstrate consistent performance, this investment can lead to greater opportunities and faster returns. The industry is responding to a demand for efficiency, and as such, we can expect to see an increasing number of prop firms offering these models.

Adapting to Market Changes and Strategies

As the prop trading landscape evolves, traders must also adapt their strategies to thrive in this changing environment. Embracing new models and being proactive about financial planning are essential components of success in this new era.

Embracing New Prop Firm Models

With the rise of immediate funding options, traders must familiarize themselves with the specifics of these new programs. Understanding the terms, conditions, and expectations of prop firms is crucial for anyone looking to take advantage of these opportunities.

Adapting to new prop firm models means being open to change. Traders should remain flexible and willing to learn about the advantages and challenges of direct funding. This may involve understanding new payout structures, trading rules, and risk management strategies that differ from traditional models. By being proactive in learning about these changes, traders can position themselves to take full advantage of the evolving landscape.

Financial Planning for Higher Costs

With the shift towards immediate funding programs, financial planning becomes even more critical. Traders must assess their budgets and be prepared for the higher initial costs associated with these opportunities.

Creating a financial plan involves evaluating the total costs of entering a prop firm's program, including any upfront fees, monthly subscriptions, or profit-sharing arrangements. It's essential to factor these costs into your overall trading strategy and ensure that you have a clear understanding of how these investments will impact your potential earnings.

Additionally, traders should consider the importance of maintaining a cushion for unexpected expenses. Trading inherently carries risks, and having a financial safety net can help traders navigate the inevitable ups and downs of the market.

Prioritize Consistency and Invest in Continuous Education

As the prop trading landscape shifts, the need for consistency and ongoing education remains paramount. Traders must prioritize building robust strategies that can withstand market fluctuations and changes in firm policies.

Consistency is key in trading, and developing a disciplined approach will help traders navigate the complexities of new funding models. This means not only adhering to trading plans but also being willing to adapt them based on performance metrics and market conditions. The ability to stick to a well-thought-out strategy, even in the face of challenges, can set successful traders apart.

Investing in continuous education is also vital in an evolving environment. As prop firms introduce new tools, platforms, and resources, traders should stay informed about best practices and emerging trends. This could involve participating in webinars, attending industry conferences, or engaging with educational materials that can enhance trading skills.

As we conclude this chapter on the future of prop trading, it's important to inspire traders to embrace the changes ahead. The evolving landscape offers new possibilities, and with it comes the opportunity for personal and professional growth.

Embracing Change and Growth

Change can be daunting, but it also brings the potential for growth. Day traders should embrace the evolution of prop trading as an opportunity to enhance their skills and expand their horizons. The shift towards immediate funding models signifies a broader acceptance of diverse trading styles and approaches.

By remaining open to new methods and strategies, traders can harness the power of change to propel their careers forward. Remember that every challenge presents an opportunity to learn and grow. Those who approach change with a positive mindset will be better equipped to navigate the complexities of the trading world.

Stay Adaptive and Consistent

In this fast-paced industry, adaptability is crucial. Traders must remain agile, ready to adjust their strategies as the market and prop firm offerings evolve. Emphasizing consistency in your trading approach will help you maintain focus and discipline, even when faced with uncertainty.

Developing a consistent routine—whether it involves daily trading rituals, regular performance reviews, or dedicated study time—can solidify a trader's foundation. Staying committed to a well-defined process will yield long-term benefits, ultimately leading to improved performance and resilience.

Your Journey is Ongoing; You Are Capable of Greatness

Finally, it's essential to recognize that your trading journey is ongoing. Whether you are a seasoned trader or just starting, remember that you have the capacity for greatness. Every trader faces challenges, but those who persevere, learn from their experiences, and adapt to change will ultimately find success.

Keep pushing forward, and don't hesitate to seek inspiration from others in the trading community. The future of prop trading is bright, and it belongs to those who are prepared to seize the opportunities that lie ahead.

Chapter 9 – Recap

- The prop trading landscape is evolving, presenting new opportunities and challenges for traders.
- Traditional evaluation-based models are giving way to immediate funding options.
- Immediate funding allows traders to access capital quickly, streamlining entry into trading.
- Higher initial costs for immediate funding programs reflect the value of quick access to capital.
- Traders must adapt strategies and familiarize themselves with new prop firm models.
- Financial planning is critical to navigate higher costs and unexpected expenses.
- Consistency in trading and ongoing education are essential for success in the changing environment.
- Embrace change as an opportunity for growth and skill enhancement.
- Stay adaptive and maintain a disciplined trading approach amidst market fluctuations.
- Remember, your trading journey is ongoing, and you possess the capacity for greatness!

Final Thoughts

As you've now reached the end of this book, remember: your journey in trading is far from over—it's just beginning. Trading is a relentless path, and success isn't granted to those who simply try; it's earned by those who endure, adapt, and thrive in the face of challenges. You've learned about the inner workings of prop firms, the strategies that help you succeed, the importance of mindset, and the discipline needed for long-term success. Now, it's time to apply this knowledge, with the confidence that each day brings you one step closer to mastery.

In this industry, there will always be market shifts, new prop firm models, and unexpected obstacles, but every challenge you face is a chance to grow stronger, sharper, and more resilient. Stay open to learning—be it through evolving trading strategies or insights gained from losses and victories alike. Prop trading is about growth, both as a trader and as an individual, pushing yourself beyond your comfort zone to unlock your potential.

Remember, the most successful traders are not those who avoided failure; they are the ones who refused to let failure define them. Keep adapting, stay humble, and trust the process. You are on the path of resilience and greatness, ready to navigate the evolving world of prop trading with courage and determination. Your journey is unique and ongoing. Embrace it fully, knowing that with persistence, you are capable of achieving remarkable things.

A Little More About the Author

KRON "THE WHITE TIGER" JENESIS

People often ask me about my nickname, *The White Tiger*. It was a name bestowed on me by my Godmother, long before I ever entered the world of trading. Somehow, it found its true resonance there. The White Tiger symbolizes a rare kind of power—one that blends strength with enigma. Tigers are natural hunters: silent, focused, patient, waiting for the right moment to strike. These are not just qualities of a tiger; they are the qualities of a true trader.

The color white adds its own magic—a symbol of clarity, a constant reminder of purpose, and a touch of the untouchable. White surrounds me, a quiet armor that sharpens my mind and keeps me grounded yet feeling light as air. To wear it is to feel a sense of invincibility, to slip into a state of clarity where precision and intuition come together seamlessly.

So, *The White Tiger* is not simply a name—it's an embodiment. It's a presence that moves beyond the charts, the trades, or the strategies, into something altogether deeper. It's more than a nickname, it's a calling.

www.ingramcontent.com/pod-product-compliance
Lightning Source LLC
Chambersburg PA
CBHW050320230526
45471CB00005B/2270